NEXT ORBIT
OF AN
ENTREPRENEUR

I0479767

INDIA · SINGAPORE · MALAYSIA

Notion Press

No.8, 3rd Cross Street
CIT Colony, Mylapore
Chennai, Tamil Nadu – 600004

First Published by Notion Press 2020
Copyright © Vikas Chandra Shah
and Narendrasingh Shekhawat 2020
All Rights Reserved.

ISBN 978-1-64919-943-0

NEXT ORBIT OF AN ENTREPRENEUR

Vikas Chandra Shah
Narendrasingh Shekhawat

INDIA · SINGAPORE · MALAYSIA

IND:CACADEMY

Indic Pledge

———◆◆———

- *I celebrate our civilisational identity, continuity & legacy in thought, word and deed.*

- *I believe our indigenous thought has solutions for the global challenges of health, happiness, peace and sustainability.*

- *I shall seek to preserve, protect and promote this heritage and in doing so,*
  - *discover, nurture and harness my potential,*
  - *connect, cooperate and collaborate with fellow seekers,*
  - *advance diversity and inclusivity in the society.*

About Indic Academy

———◆◆———

Indic Academy is a non-traditional 'university' for traditional knowledge. We seek to bring about a global renaissance based on Indic civilizational and indigenous thought. We are pursuing a multidimensional strategy across time, space and cause by establishing centers of excellence, transforming intellectuals and building an ecosystem.

Indic Academy is pleased to support this book.

I thank my friend Vikas 'cauz he believed in me at the time when I started unbelieving myself.

I thank all others close to me for their strong disbelief in me which ignited my passion to prove myself.

Why I wrote this book

Most of us in our childhood used to take notes during their class in school and memorized them for passing exams. Unfortunately Somehow we stopped taking daily notes of life to understand and pass the exam of life.

Herein in this book, I am just jotting down what all happened in my life, which ultimately made my life more meaningful. May be this reading will help you to shorten your learning curve in entrepreneurship.

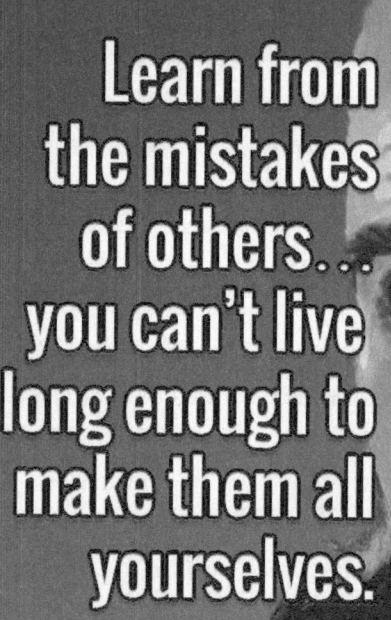

Learn from
the mistakes
of others...
you can't live
long enough to
make them all
yourselves.

- Chanakya

LIFE CHROME

You can't skip chapters,

that's not how life works. You have to
read every line, meet every character.
You won't enjoy all of it. Hell, some
chapters will make you cry for weeks.
You will read things you don't want to
read, you will have moments when you
don't want the pages to end. But you have
to keep going. Stories keep the world
evolving. Live yours, don't miss out.

Courtney Peppernill

Contents

Introduction to the Book

When I started to pen down my experiences of life in the form of this book, then many subjects ran across my mind to write upon. At first I thought I should write on "how to raise funds from VC". Then I thought of writing on "low hanging fruits" -the small opportunities that exists which an entrepreneur overlooks in search of the next big thing.

But finally I thought of writing about how to get in to the next orbit and still be happy in life. As nothing is more important in life than happiness for an entrepreneur or anyone else. More often than not during our rotation in our life orbit, while trying to jump in the next orbit we don't even feel our "happiness". And thus I landed upon the subject title of the book.

Next Orbit of an Entrepreneur

Orbit, yes we are all revolving in our own orbits the whole of our life trying to jump into the next higher orbit.

While revolving in our orbit, some of us want to jump and leapfrog the emotional hindrances and become emotionally stable. Some work hard to become financial secure and those who are secure, are in process of jumping to have abundance. A sportsperson who plays for state, spend hours and years to play national, and national players pursues happiness in becoming an international player. A college graduate dedicates his whole present to make a better future in the form of a good job. And many who get a good job want to leave their job in search of greener(seemingly) pastures of entrepreneurship.

Our aspirations keep on shifting.

Whole of our life goes in running after fulfillment of desires.

What is the next orbit of an entrepreneur?

The next orbit for an entrepreneur can be financial freedom, emotional (social freedom) or it may be the most important to be in self love.

Jumping in higher orbit never stops in life.

How does it help to know that we all are in our right orbits? When we know we are in orbits, the journey of life becomes smooth and clear.

But "by the time we understand the game of life, the game is really over."

The above philosophy of life is best explained by the following anecdote of a bear

In a jungle lived a cute bear, oblivious of the world in the lap of nature. Once when he was wading in the jungle, he slipped in a well that was covered with husk and he started sliding into the well. As he was

slipping down the well, he grabbed a twig of a tree which branched into the well. The bear held it firmly. The bear was very frightened and death was swinging in front of his eyes. Amidst this, one drop of honey fell from the same tree onto his lips. He started licking his lips and enjoyed the nectar. He forgot that he was on the verge of death.

It was not that the bear had not tasted much better nectar in the past, but it was only this time that he really cherished it. He was in absolute present. Had he feared death he would not have been able to taste the nectar. This is enlightenment, this is the divine realization.

Each of one us in reality are traversing a journey from life to death. Each of one us are so engrossed in holding on to our past or in future that we forget the pleasures of the present.

For an entrepreneur the message is -Don't be in a utopian state of achieving things. Actually you will never be able to satiate this desire to achieve. As after reaching the next orbit, you would still be wanting to achieve more, as there are endless circles of orbits to achieve. The desire will never satiate.

You as an entrepreneur, will never be satisfied with your first investment, first customer, first team. Understand these are just orbits. Things are not permanent. They are just aspirations. Don't sacrifice your happiness while you act for the future, as happiness is the sole aim of life.

To be happy in life, you need to live in the present. In each day you live, have space for everybody, your children, your parents, your wife and have space for yourself.

What people call "work life balance" needs to be understood differently in case of entrepreneurs as for them, apart from maintaining balance in personal relations and work, there is an additional axis –SELF Fulfilling desires of self in the given societal ecosystem to keep themselves happy.

I was unaware when and how my aspirations were shifting with the passage of time. Twenty five years ago I was dying to become an engineer and I bartered joy of teenage years for attaining that goal. Then I ran after doing an MBA. from achieving this I made myself restless to get good job, which I eventually got. My aspirations did not stop there. I don't remember when did the urge to be an entrepreneur started dwelling inside me. Though having a cushy corporate job, I started moving towards the murkier water of the ocean of entrepreneurship.

I started drafting business plan and darting it to VC's then a moment of truth made me realize that before making a business plan I should make "life plan", first helping myself how I would like to spend my life. Not to have three year financial projection drafted for a VC but to first plan each day. With my planning I now give slots in my daily routine slots for myself, for my family, for my parents. I am better equipped to give equal weightage to my present earnings and building future today in measured way with defined metrics. Instead of going berserk on just business aspirations, today I do daily exercise, have good nutrition, teach my children, reach home on time.

This is the balance.

My two cents to you, take out time for yourself, go on the terrace on Sundays and bask in sunshine aimlessly or go in the garden with your family. Leave your laptops or office calls when you are at home.

It is hard to do but yes we all can train yourself.

Be happy wherever you are and do not lose your happiness in worries of the future.

Lesson

****This bear accidentally slipped into the well, wherein entrepreneurs should be well aware that they are slipping in well of the perils of entrepreneurship. It is not easy as it may appear. You require a razor sharp mind and nerve of steel to crack this difficult nut.

Chapter 1

Your Dreams Too Will Change as You Progress in Life

———————✦———————

Today as I returned from the office I was sitting with my laptop to write this book and my son sprang up with a stick and asked me to hold it. My son was 10 years old and was trying to do magic by seeing tricks from a book that I bought for him.

My son Rohan performed a trick. Worries of my office got lost with the lighter side of magic tricks performed by my son and I was laughing with him. Then he said, "Papa, do you also know magic? magic hua kabhi apke sath?" (Does magic ever happen to you).

As Rohan went outside and got lost with his other flatmates, his words were reverberating in my ears "Magic Hua Kabhi?"

"No, magic never happened to me.'I said to myself,'For the last twenty years, I have been attempting to build a venture but have lost several times.' I reaffirmed this thought by reiterating to myself, 'I have made a fool of myself more than a dozen times.'

I was undergoing lots of turmoil and needed a vent.

I was lost in this whirlpool of thought and suddenly my phone started vibrating. It was swamiji, my college friend, my mentor, and a good spirit who was always ready to help me. How come I forgot about him. He called me to inform that he was visiting me at my house the same evening. I was filled with a mixture of joy and bewilderment on this. I thought I would open up all my dilemmas to him and get his opinion about it.

I was lost in my thoughts, recalling my whole life and never realized the passing time when a ring of doorbell intruded my thoughts.

Here was my mentor, my college friend Vikas at the door. As Vikas sat next to me, I shared my thoughts, "My friend, I have tried a lot. No magic has ever happened to me."

He said, "Are you sure that whenever you tried to achieve something in life, magic never happened to you."

"Yes,"I confirmed, magic never happened to me.

"You are wrong", my friend said confidently, "magic always happened to you, but you never noticed, nor appreciated. Nonetheless, tell me, where do you think you tried and no magic happened. I have my ears for you.

I started narrating,

As you know I come from a middle class family. My father was a transporter. A transport company is an intermediary which makes money on the brokerage when a truck gets a truck load from a factory. When I was in primary class, I once approached my father and said "Papa, I want to reach out to all neighbours to collect funds to make an effigy of Ravan for

Dushera and buy some crackers for it."My father though he was not well off at that time considered it very bad. As it will bring down his reputation in society. He said, "I will give you money for putting crackers in your ravan. But dare not go to anybody else".

I made a Ravan without the help of others and burnt it on dussehra. But I lost the opportunity to build and lead a team to realize my energy and creativity.

In my teen age, sometimes I used to write poems. The poems started finding places in Dainik Bhaskar –a leading newspaper of India. Once again, my father instead of appreciating my poems cool headedly told me"beta, poems say koi ghar nahi chalta" (By writing poems you can't earn your bread.)

At that time, I never realized by this discouragement I was mentally conditioned to leave my passion and be on the path where the world headed. The world where creativity struggles to find a place.

I don't hold my father responsible for this but he represented the society which runs on objects rather on emotions.

I was thus conditioned to excel in studies to achieve a richer lifestyle, as most of us do. From school days I started nursing thoughts of becoming a highly successful businessman. In my engineering days I used to stick pictures of Porsche and Lamborghini on the walls of my hostel room.

I wanted to jump from my present orbit to the next orbit of wealth through rigorous studies.

In this process, I stressed or rather burned myself so much that I once suffered from hypertension later in my life. My mind conditioning led me to this stage.

Now I realize that if one is in the stage of working hard to get a degree, a good job, a VC investment, these are not worth your happiness.

There are examples galore who started on a mission to accomplish something and jumped to the next orbit, only to realize later that there is something more interesting for them to do. Take for eg. Harsha Bhogle who did post graduation from IIM -Ahmedabad after graduating in engineering. He finally turned his career as writer and cricket commentator.

It is not only Harsha that I have observed, following is a set of few persons who changed their orbit and the course of their life. **Summing up, what seems most compelling today may be quite irrelevant tomorrow. Everything changes. So, be calm and just observe things which happen and act without unduly worrying about it and overthinking.**

These examples are of my MBA mates who changed their direction from the orbit of societal conditioning to the orbit of passion.

1. Kalyan Chakroborty is an engineer who studied MBA with me. After spending a few years in the corporate world he left the job. He now runs an NGO in a small village in Andhra working for the upliftment of the poor.

2. Sarvimeet Singh Oberoi is another engineer who studied MBA with me. He started his career as a

Marketing manager at HCL and was later VP at Radio Mirchi. It must have been a gruelling process to reach where he was. But he also left the corporate ladder. He is a animal lover and now runs his own company Petfelix -a daycare company for dogs. He is there Chief Dog officer.

3. Nitin Pandey is another engineer who studied MBA with me and quit his corporate job to take a plunge in entrepreneurship.

4. Aneesh another engineer who studied MBA with me quit his government job at a Navratna PSU. Because he didn't find any challenge in his job. If I remember correctly he said he needed a kick.

It is not that they became financially independent in the first few months of their job that they were able to make financial decisions to quit their corporate career. In fact many of the above mentioned persons may still be under tremendous financial pressure owing to entrepreneurship but it is only that they broke the chain and now are in the next orbit of passion by listening to self.

These examples are mentioned here to tell you not to worry about their future and do not worry about placements. In fact what you want to achieve today, tomorrow you would like to leave the same thing. Don't fret if your desired result does not come your way.

Quite possible in future, you may follow your natural instincts and not society obligations.

You do not know your next orbit so just be in the present. There is an element in your life called society which may be your parents, your friends or your teachers -they all shape your thoughts and influence. It is only when you develop the understanding of the way they are shaping your life, you are able to control your destiny. This comes with constant observation. To be self, takes time, sometimes it never happens, for someone it happens early in life. That is your next orbit. It requires energy.

Lesson

Chapter 2

Be Patient with Your Dreams Even if it Takes 20 Years or More

In 1999, 21 years ago when I was in engineering college, I started preparing for my MBA entrance exam. I took help of a coaching centre to prepare for GD PI (group discussion and personal interview) for an MBA. At the coaching centre I was mentored on "how to crack the interview". I was asked what subject do you want to choose to major in -marketing, finance or HR. I said,"finance". I was asked "well then, what in finance do you aspire to?" I told them that I like number crunching and investments as a theme but I don't know what all avenues are there in Finance. They said I need to prepare an answer for "What do you want to become as a finance professional.", what will you say. I told my mentor "Sir there are so many fields in finance which I don't even know. I equally like all spheres of finance. I can become a Venture capitalists, a consultant, a banker, a CFO. How can I tell beforehand. But my mentor said, Naren, you need to research on one subject. So that when you are asked on the subject you should be able to answer all of them. They suggested me to take Equity Analyst as a preferred role to do in career. I prepared myself accordingly. I prepared my script and rehearsed it.

I wanted to do an MBA from a tier-1 college. I cleared the written exams of few prestigious colleges like IISc Bangalore. IISc has only 18 seats for post graduate program in management and out of that only 9 seats were general. I cleared the written exam of it and was fortunate enough to get a interview call from it. During the interview one of the interviewers asked me what do you want do in life.

I responded without a second's thought "Sir, I want to do business."

He asked me what kind of business?

I was aware of the success story of Amazon at that time and I promptly responded to them saying " E-commerce"

The interviewer asked " What are the types of e-commerce models?"

I did not know the answer at that time. I kept mum.

I was not selected. Perhaps not knowing this answer was a turning point.

This was in 1999, Flipkart was founded in 2007.

I was repenting that I could not secure an admission in any of the IIMs despite my hard work. No magic happened. I worked very hard."

My friend opened his dairy and jotted down surreptitiously,

"Naren was fortunate enough to complete engineering but there are many who have to leave even the primary education due to family conditions. He is not reflecting back in life by thanking God in the pursuit of his next orbit."

My friend then turned towards me and said

"Naren, do you remember something more"looking intently he continued,"When you got admission, can you recollect if there was anybody who was not taken in or was rejected."

"Yes," I said. I vividly it was the year 2000, I was appearing for the interview for the entrance of management college which I finally graduated from. Along with other interviewees I was sitting in a big hall of that college. I noticed a girl who seemed to be very tense sitting next to me in the hall. Her fingers were crossed literally. I was calm and was not very excited about this college. To break the ice I asked her, "which college have you graduated from?" She said, "Lady Shriram College of Commerce." A very reputed college, I said to myself. She told me that it was her second attempt for entrance at this B-School. I remember through the emails we exchanged later and came to know that she was not selected, whereas I got selected in this college. Though I was selected in this college but took it as a failure the whole of my life as being devoid of a non-IIM tag.

My friend noted in a piece of paper covering from me and wrote **"Selected in a premier B-School and still not happy."**

This is a missing tile syndrome. (Read Dennis Prager theory)

Missing Tile Syndrome -a term coined by Dennis Prager

Imagine yourself, sitting in a newly constructed room. You look up and you see such a perfect tile ceiling. However, while you are admiring its ceiling, you notice one tile is missing. From there on, no matter how beautiful the ceiling is, you can't fully enjoy its beauty just because of one single missing tile. So you finally called the maintenance and had the missing tile replaced. After that, you now have the perfect ceiling once again.

Now, let me shift your concentration on our lives today. All of us have something that we don't have. Those are the missing tiles in our lives. However, there are just some tiles that no matter how hard you try, it can never be replaced or fixed. These missing tiles in the ceiling can be replaced and once again make the ceiling look perfect. But sadly, there is no such thing as a **PERFECT life**. You will never come to the point that your ceiling will all have the tiles.

There is a big DANGER when you concentrate on the missing tiles in your life. It can make you dissatisfied, ungrateful, remorseful, and unhappy. At this point in time, you might be suffering from the Missing Tile Syndrome.

"The Missing Tile Syndrome" is a term coined by Dennis Prager. It simply means focusing on the things that we don't have and in the process, robbing ourselves of happiness.

The following excerpt is from bible which says,

Avoid Covetousness

"Let your conduct be without **COVETOUSNESS**; be content with such things as you have. For he Himself has said, "I will never leave you nor forsake you."" (Ibrews 13:5)

What is covetousness? It is the strong desire to acquire something that belongs to other people. If you notice, covetousness starts with the mind. Though some people might not see your thoughts, the desire to have something can become too strong, that you've always been thinking about it, that your words and action made it obvious.

Covetousness can be deceitful because you can never have enough of what you covet. It is also damaging to one's life because of its insatiable cravings. Finally, covetousness can lead to other sins such as **stealing, lying, adultery, murder, and the list just goes on and on.**(from www. becomingchristians. com)

This covetousness only led Ramalinga Raju to embezzle 1. 5 billion USD from Satyam Computers, Naresh Goyal to siphon huge amounts of money abroad from Jet, Singh brothers of Ranbaxy siphon huge amounts of money from their company. The desire to have more never satiates and the greed to have more never lets you from being happy.

While studying in the B-School there were many questions we students pondered upon all which were centered towards making money.

We asked our faculty members during our first year of studies, which stream gets the highest package in this college, finance or marketing?

I never listened to the inner self. I kept on changing my path according to the reality of the world my seniors projected to us. When companies came for placement I kept on customizing CVs to adjust it according to the kind of companies that came on campus for placement. When a FMCG company came to campus I wrote the CV objective statement "I want to make a career in FMCG ". And to a bank, I would say I liked banking as a sector. To jump in the next orbit, I was ready to dance to the tunes of people. And we all do that? Don't we?

I never thought of my happiness and my passion in doing a thing and taking a stand for it while choosing a company. I always wanted others to choose me. This continued later in my life when I approached VCs as an entrepreneur. I wanted to do everything which fit in their investment criteria.

Many make a frequent rollover in changing companies to just justify their hunger for a higher package.

I had a question whether I should change companies or should stick on to a company for long. Barely few look for the culture of a company to join, and most of the time it is just a salary package that matters to us. We stick to our conditioning for financial gains at the cost of personal growth and humane development.

Following is a best example of how we can start discovering yourself detaching from the thoughts which were initially induced to us. Quoted here verbatim is a statement of Phaninandra Sama -Founder of Redbus from his interview in LiveMint. When he says, he stopped and reflected back to see, is it OK to travel a beaten path, a path well trodden by all others or to take a stand of own.

> *"There are so many things I'd have never realized, if not for entrepreneurship, and never introspected. I changed a lot during the past seven years. I used to bribe people, I used to be this angry young man. Today, I'm more tolerant and much higher on values."*
>
> **— Phanindra Sama, -founder of REDBUS**

This resilience of not taking money or giving money as bribe is not easy. This jump in the next orbit comes with time and practice.

Listen to your heart. It says something to you which you tried to suppress many times. Whole of our life we get evaluated by others in society early by parents, then by teachers, by friends, by college interviewers, by company interviewers, by investors and your life is led by everybody else except you.

We never speak out of our heart because of societal pressure and conditioning.

That is the inertia of your current orbit which holds where you are and that is the amount of resilience it needs to jump in the next orbit.

One is made to understand that if one speaks the truth on his likings, he will be left out by society.

Society downplays us. For our society, money is important which we easily can relate to and hence we follow it.

We are so fixated in our orbit that we do not have enough daring to challenge the established norms. We dance to the tunes of the society and the surroundings.

Create your own steps and dance to your own tune, no matter how funny it may seem.

Lesson

Chapter 3

If You are a First Time Entrepreneur, Find an Investor in Your Own City

In the year 2002 when I was in the final semester of MBA, once there was a poster on the notice board announcing free entry to B-School students on the first ever TIE summit at ITC Delhi. I had to google 'what is TIE'" and came to know that it is an organization named "The Indus Valley Entrepreneurs".

Since the entry was free and I wanted to become an entrepreneur I made it a point to attend this event.

I was dot on time at the venue in my best formal attire and entered the hall, where venture clinics were going on. I enrolled myself to attend one and came out on the lawn where the IAS officers of Haryana and Punjab government were on mikes, pitching their state as the best place to invest, promising one window clearance. I kept on hopping from one group of people to another, to just get a hang of what is going on. What is the junta talking about?" I mused. In one corner, I found a person who resembled CK Prahalad and in another I saw someone resembling Narayan Murthy. I nudged people to get into this group and realized that there were actually CK

Prahlad and Narayan Murthy. It seemed that now business was very easy, there were investors, the governments and mentor clinics, so easy that it appeared that they were waiting for me.

One elegantly dressed lady in her early twenties observing me, came near me and introduced herself as Geetika Dayal. She handed me the business card which read Executive Director TIE Delhi and asked me about myself. I was a bit taken aback and told her that I am here on an open invitation for the program to represent my B-School. She told me that the correct way of meeting someone is to give a brief 10 second introduction which should include one's name, background and purpose for talking and preferably exchange his card during the conversation.

My friend opened his diary and again made a remark, "Naren has learnt how to introduce himself. This is a part of grooming which many B-Schools don't teach". Many people get old but they do not know how to properly open up a conversation.

I thereafter entered the venture clinic where there were two gentlemen representing a company named Hewitt. One of the consultants asked, "Okay Mr., what do you want to start?"

Before this I had met the founder of Parsec Technologies - a successful call centre company. And I told the consultant without giving a second thought, "I want to start a call centre."

The gentleman further probed with questions like, "What kind of a call centre, domestic or international? Who would be your target client? How many seater call centres? How much investment is required, what is the estimated revenue and expenditure, who all are the prospective team members who would execute this?"

I was not prepared for all these questions. All I had an idea was of a call centre. The gentleman nodded amongst themselves and said, "Go and work in the industry for some time and remember in life that the first outside investment will always come from someone who is close to you and who is close to see the project happening. Start after some years."

The first investment (angel investment or the seed capital) is generally given on your face value and not on the project. And investor would want to see the execution right under his nose.

Pick an investor from your place and do the venture in your own city

Lesson

Chapter 4

Luck is Nothing but Persistence

The story is of the year 2002, when I was graduating from my B-School in Delhi. It was recession time and we were a batch of 120 people to be placed. There were fewer companies and lesser known companies coming on campus than the previous year due to recession in the industry. And by the end of of placement season only 50-60 percent candidates were placed. As days passed by, candidates were losing hope whether any more companies will be coming to the campus. Then there was an announcement made by the college administration and hostel warden that March end would be the last working day of the college. Only one month was left for the candidates to get the placement. With passage of time the students now started accepting jobs with salary as low as Rs 15, 000/- per month against their peers who were placed in blue chip companies with hefty pay packages ranging around Rs 60, 000/- per month. Such a huge gap it was. I was also one of the unlucky fellows who was yet to be placed. There was gloominess and tense environment all around.

Then to try my luck, I started daily visiting the placement office and noted down addresses of HR corporates and with a covering letter, I started posting my CV via snail mail to 10 companies a day. I took up a challenge and decided I will not go for a 12, 000/- or 15, 000/- job because once I accept it I will not be allowed to sit for the next company as a policy rule of the college. Finally, we had to vacate the hostel and many students who had come to study in this college from far off places like Kolkata and Chennai went back home empty handed without a job. But I chose to live outside the campus waiting for companies which were coming once a week or once a fortnight.

Then came my present employer and it hired me with a heftier package to my surprise.

The interesting part of the story is that when I was on my first posting at Kolkata, I received a correspondence from the HR department of Escorts Mutual Fund stating that I have been selected for joining their company. Escorts Mutual Fund was one of the companies to whom I had posted my CV in a cold call fashion. Here my "luck" (which is nothing but persistence with tweaking the approach every time) worked - had I not stayed back I wouldn't have got my present employer. **The key is to hang on when times are tough,** by refusing petty jobs and aim at the best and very often one gets best.``

My friend jotted in his dairy

"Magic happened and things worked for Naren. His father allowed him to stay back in Delhi when other students left, This is overlooked by him. Many students have to leave their studies when they meet unexpected happenings in their family."

It was not magic or luck but hard work and luck which played together so never mind if your luck sometimes doesn't not work. Hard work will bring luck.

The harder you work and persistent you are, the luckier you get.

Lesson

Chapter 5

How to Manage Personal Finance

I have been investing in the stock market since my childhood.

I remember I even once travelled from my engineering college in Maharashtra to Jaipur Rajasthan just to compel my father to invest in a particular IPO of a company. The company was Rajshree Polyfill. It was a Birla group company and was a 100 % export oriented company-a big thing in those times. Such was my craziness to make money.

When I used to invest with my father, I used to advise him and invest mostly in IPOs. With my insistence he got in to trading of shares in secondary market. But he started losing money. It was the time of my sister's marriage and he lost all his money in the stock market. Fortunately one of his businesses clicked and he could manage the marriage decently.

With this he distanced himself from the stock market.

But my charm in stocks remained undwindled. I have heard stories of Warren Buffet, Rakesh Jhunjhunwala, Damani who made fortunes on bourses.

I was so charmed by their success in stock market that I took a personal loan of Rs 10 Lakh to invest in stock market.

I found many experts who were making money in multibagger stocks, I googled on net and searched for multibaggers. Multibagger is a term meaning stocks which give manifold returns and are emerging bluechip companies.

EPS, PE, Book Value were not new terms to me as I used to make investments based on these in IPO by reading their IPO application forms since my childhood. And knowledge drives the fear away. Though it was half knowledge as in stock market there was more than technicals that drive the stock market and it was fundamentals.

Another factor which prompted me to invest was investment advisors who said to invest in equities when you are in your thirties as you can take risk and in old age one should go for investment in debt instruments.

I once again started buying Capital Market and Dalal Street magazine. Getting up early in the morning with a remote in my hand and putting CNBC on at 9:15 in became my daily routine. I started reading technical charts, upward and downward trends of stocks. I thought I can time the market by selling and buying at the right time. But I was proved to be wrong. And nothing worked. I was losing money. Though not only my family even my friends termed it as crime to gamble in stock market, but I was adamant. I lost money in day trading but even this couldn't constrain my charm of the stock market from mind. I thought there is a problem with my approach and I changed my strategy and became a long term investor. I heard to sit tight on the stocks and be a long term investor.

One stock advisory was able to convince me that I made losses because I was investing on my own. They told me that as when we have a medical problem we go to a doctor and for legal issues we go to a lawyer. Similarly I need a stock advisory firm who is expert in creating wealth. I invested another 5 lakhs on their advice. I bought shares of Rain Industries and Tata Motors amongst others. Shares of Rain Industries slided steeply and whole capital got eroded while I remained invested.

Then one day my elder brother called me and said,

"Naren, do you know that investing in shares is like an addiction and a person always thinks I will make a killing in the next move.

I got convinced and said "OK I will stop it. "

He said, when?

I said, once I am able to recover my losses and the stocks rise once again.

I said, this is like a cigarette in your hand and it will drop only when you immediately let it go by opening your fingers. You need to do it now. Now or never.

This time, not only I heard it but adhered to it. I sold my old stocks that very moment, though in loss and came out of the stock market once and for all.

I learnt the following lessons.

1. **Never invest in shares directly yourself or on a stock advisory's firm. Invest only when you have it in spare which even if you lose it won't affect your financial health. You can opt for mutual funds.(If you are a layman and not a professional)**

2. **Never take a loan to invest.**

Lesson

My two cents to you, people will give you gyan on wealth created by Rakesh Jhunjhunwala, Warren Buffet or Radha Krishan Damania. But remember that they have devoted, huge amount of time and dedication to get to the level of success they have today (For eg. Warren Buffet reads more than 500 pages of financial reports including annual reports a day!!!!). Compare yourself with amount of time and herculean efforts likes of RK and Damania have put, this will help you to resist the temptation of investing in shares. Not only you will lose money, you will lose your breath with ups and downs of stocks, unless you are seasoned in making profits. And if you want to test yourself invest a little amount and check your investments not for few months and rotate it for a year at least to see if you are able to generate profits constantly.

Indian stock regulators do not care anything about investors' loss.

The same holds true for entrepreneurship, you see big players like Jef Bezos and want to emulate. But are unaware of their dedication, devotion and hardships, which is fun to them. But it can be a pain in your ass.

Following are the examples which support my theory that fundamentals rule and not technicals in stock price. Many of the following bluechip companies failed that included esteemed business house of Ambanis or brands like Jet or Gitanjali Gems, Satyam Computers or Yes Bank. They are all Category A companies audited by Big 5. If you would have made a portfolio in these stocks you would have doomed.

Following table shows all time high and all time low share prices (dated January 2020) of randomly chosen bluechip companies that have failed in the past.

Company Name	All Time High	All Time Low
Yes Bank	400	20
Jet Airways	1500	20
Cafe Coffee Day	300	20
Satyam Computers	3000	10
Gitanjali Gems	**600**	**1**
DLF	1000	130
RCap	**3000**	**4**
RInfra	3000	9
RPower	**450**	**1**

What is recommended to buy is based on technical charts which are taught in school and not company fundamentals. And when fundamentals of bluechip companies like Satyam Computers and Yes Bank go awry, then the message is clear that not to bet on individual stocks.

Some one will put in extra "dimag" to read EBDIT, PAT, Industry PE to become an investment expert, what they fail to understand is corporate fraud, government regulations, country's civil status, US federal policy can topsy turvy their knowledge and devastate (yes devastate) your goal of financial freedom.

When I lost money in stocks, then I reflected on what is the correct way of building wealth.

Generally we have the following three investment options in life.

1.   Gold
2.   Property
3.   Stocks

To some intellectuals additional dimensions are investing in

1.   Oil
2.   Forex
3.   Startups

Now, this time I was out of the stock market. As I knew this is a danger zone for me. I invested only in Mutual funds that took only a part of monthly savings.

Comparing returns from Gold and Equities

BusinessToday.In

RETURNS IN THE LAST 10 YEARS

Year	Gold	Sensex	Silver
2019	24.1	14.1	22.9
2018	7.5	5.9	-2.1
2017	5.2	27.5	-1.5
2016	11.5	2	19.9
2015	-6.2	-5	-7.9
2014	-8.2	29.6	-15.6
2013	-4.9	8.5	-24.3
2012	12.1	25.1	12.1
2011	31.7	-25.1	8.8
2010	23.6	17.4	71

*% change on a calendar year basis

Returns

From Business Today Magazine

Gold investors have reaped slightly better returns than investors in the stock market this decade. BSE Sensex has appreciated by 130% in the last 10 years and gold has given 134% returns.

When you compare the returns, over a period of 10 years (the compounded growth rate) gets averaged out and in 10 years the return is nearly the same. But the results are different if you put a lump sum amount in one year and may vary drastically and may even go in negative.

Gold will never give you zero returns. Your capital will never get eroded.

Investing directly in shares may give you zero return. It is safe to invest in equities via mutual funds and that too through SIP. One should start early in career investing in SIP, smallest could be 500, and on the higher side, it could be anything.

Property-Generally property comes in large value. At least more than Rs 20 lakh in any case. It could turn out to be a gamble of one's life if it doesn't perform. Your property may give you negative returns also. Capital may get depreciated but not get eroded completely. It may turn illiquid as it depends upon a buyer and it may be hard to find a buyer when you want to sell.

The lessons are

1. **Never put all your investment in one asset class out of Gold, Property and Stocks. Spread them evenly in these classes. Have a balanced asset allocation in property, gold and stocks.**

2. **While investing in Stocks, never do investment on your own and choose investment via SIP mode of Mutual Fund.**

3. **While investing in Gold, one is advised to choose a Gold ETF fund.**

4. **One should not invest in property by taking a loan. Though you may be influenced by income tax gains and bank loans to build an asset.) This EMI if you use otherwise in MF will fetch you better returns.**

Chapter 6

Difference between
Wealth and Money

I was very clear on the difference between wealth and money. **Income** is the annual earning that one makes at the job while **wealth** is the value one gets from the assets he owns.

Wealth can be created in two ways either by owning shares of a company or by having a company of yours.

I got disillusioned with investing in stocks after losing all my precious earnings at a very young age. Media platforms like Your story, Economic times were daily filed with umpteen stories of startups and becoming unicorns very fast. These media platforms were flooded with news of funding from Matrix Partners, Sequoia and Softbank which society took as validation of success. And it intoxicates society so much that they lure the newcomer entrepreneurs and sometimes mislead them too. As it seemed that you only need an idea and free money is on the table which alas! is not true.

I too was getting tempted to start off in the dream world of entrepreneurship.

Chapter 7

Don't Give Undue
Importance to Equity

It was in 2006 that I was toying with the idea of making a B2C travel portal. I wanted it be the fourth largest travel portal in India after Makemytrip, Yatra and Cleartrip. I had knowledge of travel API and GDS and airline reservations. I thought I would make a B2C travel portal. I approached Darshan Bhai owner of All 5 Season Travels - a leading travel agency at Mumbai. Though I approached many travel agents but he responded positively when I sought investment to start the venture. I planned to leave my job as soon as I get the investment. I made a business plan which required an investment of Rs 1 crore. It was only third year of my service in the corporate sector as an employee and I did not have any savings. I told Darshan Bhai that I do not have anything to invest and if he could invest Rs 1 crore. He studied my plan, called me for a meeting and said "Look, I can invest 1 Crore as per your plan but we will have to make an agreement.

Without giving a second thought I said, "I am ready."

He said,"Be patient and listen first," and continued,"I will invest Rs 1 Crore out of which Rs 50 lakh will be my equity and rest Rs 50 lakh will be a debt to you which I will recover as soon as the company churns profit." he further asked me, "Now tell me, is it fine?"

I was baffled. I couldn't understand this rider and asked him, "Darshan Bhai, do I have some time?"

I smiled and said,"You have all the time in the world. I'm in no hurry."

I went home and, in the evening, I called up my father who was in Jaipur and narrated the incident to him and asked for his advice. My father said,"it is 50:50 deal what extra are you getting for your talent and hard work that you are going to put in. My father sounded perfect to my understanding. Next day I appeared in front of Darshan Bhai and said that I am not getting my due share from the deal. Darshan Bhai didn't utter a word and offered me coffee. The meeting ended and I left. Thereafter, I kept on pursuing him over phone and mail but the damage was done.

My friend discreetly noted and made a remark in his dairy

"Magic happened to Naren at an early age of 26, he was getting an investment of one crore rupees which he did not realize at that time."

Closing the dairy, my friend faced me and said,

"Naren, you should have accepted the deal and moved ahead. When you are a first time entrepreneur, do not get stuck on equity. A player is given the chance to play the next innings if he plays the first inning well."

When you are a first time entrepreneur, do not give undue weightage to the percent of equity you are getting. Because if you are able to execute and build one company, you will have another chance, where you will be able to dictate your terms.

Don't leave the deal as a first entrepreneur, you may repent it for lifetime.

Lesson

Sachin Binsal is given a next chance. He is being invested with crores of rupees in his second entrepreneurial attempt at Navi Technologies (a fintech venture) after he executed his first company Flipkart well.

Alok Mittal who sold his first company Jobsahead to Monster, is now on to founding his next venture -Indifi.

Kunal Shah -Investors have funded him for his next venture Cred even before he rolled out the product, just because they knew he could execute.

Sachin, Kunal and Alok are not accidental serial entrepreneurs, they are playing their second innings or we can say they are in their next orbit only because they played well in the first innings.

You need to have the right approach with your investors, your cofounders, employees and business partners.

When you are a first time entrepreneur, dilute your majority stake if required and do not hang your company's fate for your own selfish moto.

Case Study : Snapdeal Merger with Flipkart.

THE ECONOMIC TIMES

Flipkart acquisition of Snapdeal collapses as latter decides to go ahead alone

BY ET BUREAU | UPDATED: AUG 07, 2017, 02:54 PM IST

NEW DELHI | BENGALURU: Jasper Infotech has terminated negotiations for the proposed sale of its troubled online marketplace Snapdeal to market leader Flipkart on Monday, ending nearly seven months of tumultuous discussions initiated by its largest investor SoftBank.

Snapdeal said that it will pursue an "independent path", while the Japanese internet and telecom conglomerate said in a statement that "we respect the decision", bringing the curtains down on a protracted saga that was once expected to result in the largest buyout in India's high-profile startup sector.

The collapse of the talks between Flipkart and Snapdeal was first reported by ET in its July 31 edition.

Snapdeal refused merger with Flipkart :Now Snapdeal market share is 1 % from a high of 25 %. One need to learn, when to hold on equity dilution and when to let loose. Had snapdeal accepted Flipkart' offer, he could have given a wonderful exit to his investors and to himself of course.

Continuing my story, I said, "In hindsight, I see my father was wrong in his judgement."

My friend noted down,

"Naren's father was not wrong. We have to understand that an advice is an opinion of other's experience. It may or may not work in your case. Always take advice with a pinch of salt. Instead of following others advice blindly it's better to delve into your instinct and act accordingly.

I continued,

I am repenting on my decision now that I missed the opportunity. I occasionally think that had I got Rs 1 Cr in 2006, I would have become another "Yatra." And it would not have taken 20 years for me to come out of a corporate job.

My friend said "**No decision is bad, no decision is good**" -It is how one perceives it.

It's not about what you have missed or what mistakes you have committed but it's about whether you have learned your lesson or not.

My friend told me that if you look at Yatra. com, it is in even losses and the same is in the process of getting sold to Ebix now. So what is the big deal about. Why do you have a sense of "missing out".

The only lesson in the whole process is that you should trust your instincts and you should be careful while acting upon someone else's experience, be it even your father.

Every one from whom you ask for advice will tell their own experience, their mind conditioning relevant to their current orbit. And it differs from person to person.

The successful people think differently and all failed people think alike.

Choose carefully who you are taking inputs from.

My friend said,

Naren, it makes no difference whether you get the funding or not or whether you would have started your entrepreneurial journey. So, do not repent it and regret and ruin your happiness.

The only thing it would have made is nothing but only confidence. By taking the funding you could have risen in one level by "managing the show", that is it.

I continued narrating my story to my friend,

The year was 2006 and I was 29 years of age. With two professional degrees, some corporate experience, lot of business ideas and energy. After I dropped my plan of launching a travel portal, I came across an advertisement of Nirma Labs in an issue of Business World magazine inviting applications from wannabe entrepreneurs.. Nirma labs was a business incubator in Ahmedabad running six month residential program for entrepreneurs. This seemed to be an another chance given to me to satiate my desires to build a venture. I applied for the program and was finally selected to join, I had to leave my job and I was ready for it.. But my father was dead against leaving my secured job. I had no conviction and confidence in myself and I relied more on my father's experience. I bowed down to his decision. After the initial years, the incubator got shut down. My father upon knowing this proudly profoundly proclaimed, "Look didn't I tell you that this would destroy your career?

My friend noted down in his dairy,

Naren did not learn from his past mistakes. An entrepreneur does not have the luxury to repeat the mistakes.

He faced me and told me,

Naren, nobody can guide you in your journey. There will be many times when you will not be having answers. If it is knowledge then try to have it but if it is advice, trust your instincts and you have to take risks.

I continued,

But before shutting down, Nirma labs gave birth to two startups which remarkingly did well. These were: Axio Biosolutions and Anaxee Technologies.

(Axio Biosolutions is a biomedical company which is now funded by Matrix partners, and Anaxee Technologiesis a biometric company is an another spin off from Nirma Labs who successfully got patent for its product)

I told my friend that since so many years I have been trying but couldn't get anywhere..

My friend said you have still not understood.

My friend said "Naren, what makes you repent and think that you have been trying and have not got results. Did this process not teach you the power of resilience. The power to withstand failures."

There is no right or wrong decision. Do your karma and do not have fear of "I am losing time".

The whole game is to overcome two emotions: greed and fear

Inaction makes you numb.

Lesson

If you are an entrepreneur, beware of whom you are taking advice. They may have imagination constraints. Go ahead and make a decision with your gut. Don't think you are 20 years of age or have 20 years of experience to guide you. Never be biased to obey those who are older to you in experience.

Chapter 8

You are Free to Flirt with Many Ideas before Choosing One

———— ✳ ————

I started thinking of starting a venture. I started googling keywords like "ideas for startups", "funded startups in US", latest startups", to get an idea of what I could start. I found many ideas and built many castles in air. Possibly, I was looking for an idea to copy and waited for years to start (as if I had infinite time) –Read Taylor's Principle in this book page number 85)

I briefed my friend while sitting next to each other sipping coffee and said "I am tired of searching for ideas."

My friend said,"**Why don't you look for ideas around yourself. You will find plenty.**" Then he excused himself hurriedly and left my home as if he deliberately wanted me to ponder on things.

I was sitting and thinking how foolish I was to call my friend and ask for his help.

I was tense and felt that life was passing by and I could not afford to waste a single minute.

Chapter 9

Few Startup Ideas

Construction

My friend Rohit was in the construction business. Rohit called me up today and told me that he got a new contract of Rs 1 crore to repair a building. But he said he is stuck with a problem. He said now with this contract he will face a challenge to get masons, civil workers, painters and civil workers. These masons migrate from one construction site to another after completion.

I asked, "Isn't it easy to get labour?"

Rohit said, "No as the demand and supply problem is in every business. Now when I am successful in creating the demand, I am facing bottleneck at the supply of resources."

Since I was busy thinking of "the next big idea", I paid little heed to my friend's problem.

The same evening it occurred to me that in fact it would be a good idea to connect the idle labor (masons) with the contractors through an app.

On googling to find out the state of masons in India, I came to know that India's construction labour force is estimated at 30 million people; about half are women. Women are rarely found in male-dominated skilled trades like carpentry, masonry, plumbing, electrical wiring etc. Even if 1 % of this workforce which is 3 lakh is assumed to get connected to a new project under construction via the app, the opportunity was huge.

The contractor would easily give Rs 200 per mason which translates into 6 crore revenue which is a handsome amount in a year.

My friends' problem now seemed to be a great opportunity and a business idea to me.

Mason app is still a good opportunity to be explored by entrepreneurs.

Lesson

Another Idea in Construction

When my friend discussed this opportunity to me, at the back of my mind I had doubts on its scalability. But these are small low hanging fruits which can help an entrepreneur to jump into the next higher orbit. As when one cracks a small business he becomes better equipped to jump for a next higher business venture.

As even Kiran Mazumdar of Biocon had once said

"Build your big dream, in one step at a time"

Many want to make a big venture in their first attempt. But one small success in a small venture equips you for the next big leap in the next orbit.

Another opportunity which was discussed by my friend Rohit was interior designing. When people think of making furniture custom designed to a house, they work merely on 2D drawing to imagine the layout and nothing is there to see the 3D visualisation before they actually choose an interior design format out of a few different layouts, colour, shades and design.

He said just think that the dimensions of a house are given of which interior is to be designed. Now just allow AR (augmented reality) and VR (virtual reality) helps a person to visualize the final structure of interiors.

He said this is possible and people are ready to buy this solution.

Another idea in Construction

Rohit once also came to me discussing his problem on maintaining accounts. This also seems to be interesting for entrepreneurs to start.My friend is a one man show.

He said," I bought Zoho as Tally is too costly for my business."

I asked him," How much is the difference?"

He said, "Zoho's cost is Rs 3000 per year and Tally is Rs 18000 one time and yearly extra charged if you opt for updates.And thus purchased Zoho because of its cost and availability on cloud. But after purchasing Zoho I had to switch to Tally and had to buy it as his accountant was not used to Zoho and it was new to him, wherein his accountant previously worked on Tally."

Lesson: Notwithstanding the growing market share of Zoho, if people are finding Zoho difficult enough to use and switch to Tally, it is for an entrepreneur to listen to.

Next my friend told me that he faces difficulty in maintaining a daily account of cash transactions he makes to his labour and vendors.

I told him there are many new apps like Khata Book and OK Credit that are doing it.

He said the market is huge and can accept other new players as well.

Business Idea in Recruitment

There are gaps in recruitment sector as well which if harnessed by an entrepreneur can bear bountiful profits. Let us assume there are only two kinds of tech products in the job portal for discussion purposes, Naukri. com (database search) and Olx (job listing). Naukri. com represents the likes of Monster, Shine and Times Job.

Naukri is darling of Mutual Fund Portfolio managers as it is a cash cow, year over year with literally no competition. But in my opinion there is a scope of new business venture in recruitment portal.

Let me discuss it here. There are two ways of hiring a candidate at Naukri. com - a **'Job Post'** and **Resdex** which is a database of crores of job seekers. Since in Redex an employer is able to see set of database (Resdex has a resume database of 5 crore jobseeker.), it scores above Job Post feature as the reach is limited. Hence Resdex commands a premium and is priced nearly three times than Naukri's 'Job Post'

Resdex is serving purpose for big organizations who use placement agencies to provide manpower or those who have in house HR teams to recruit and have frequent requirements.

For SME with 5-25 employees run by one or two people there is no easy way out and there is a pain point. These micro enterprises have to pay a huge sum of money on resdex (more than three time of Naukri Job Posting). The employer has to go through the pain of reviewing 100's of CV and pay a higher price even when the market is buyer dominated (where jobs are scarce). He has to filter candidates manually, send them messages, click their responses individually, negotiate their salary and arrange for an interview.

These all tasks can be done by a RPO which is nothing but Recruitment job portal which does end to end function on a tech platform. If an app is made to ease the pain of SME recruitment, I am sure there is enough market for it.

Though the job listing platforms like OLX and Quikr are there but in absence of complete RPO they are not serving the purpose. (As OLX and Quikr have to cater to other classifieds as well.)

Another idea in Online truck broking business

Before discussing the opportunity in the trucking sector let me make you familiar with three factors on which road transportation depends. It depends upon the shipper (factory owner), the transporter (broker) and the truck owners.

In my school days, my father was a transporter who acted as a brokerage house between a truck owner and a factory owner or a shipper. These brokers earn a commission in matching the shipper and the truck owners. I remember, we siblings used to daily surreptitiously check my father's ledger when he returned back from office.

We used to check for the word "Katoti" in his daily ledger. The word "katoti" is used for the arbitrage opportunity that existed between rate given to truck owners and rate received from shippers. Normally he used to charge Rs 200 for small truck from truck owners and Rs 700 per bigger truck. But in Katoti sometimes he used to manage making money as much ten times (a great sum those days) of his normal commission. This Katoti was a trade secret and was closely guarded.

Now, when I was searching for business ideas, I thought it would be good idea to connect directly the factory owners and with the truck owners, removing the brokers would be good idea. I was induced to this thinking because MakeMyTrip kind of OTA's replaced the offline travel agents to a great extent and Zerodha kind of online platforms replaced agents in the offline stock market. But there is a fallacy in this thought.

Truck Transport startups like LetsTranport, Blowhorn, Lotrucks, TruckSuvidha and TruckGuru are all operating on the same model i. e. removing the truck broker and connecting the factory owner and the truck owner directly through their problem.

But I have to come to understand that this model which worked in the travel and share market is not working as desired in road transport startups. The way these startups are operating is that they give fixed quotes to factory owners based upon estimation. Once a query is received for a truck from a factory owner these startups arrange for a truck at the backend offline. These startups are leveraging technology primarily to generate leads online. It is nearly impossible to maintain inventory of trucks online because of huge operations complexity.

They are not operating as pure technology play.

One doable and feasible startup idea is to just connect factory owners to brokers. (As factory owners dominate, being a buyers market, they would prefer to get lower rates by getting different bids for trucks required from brokers.) Of Course this would work for small enterprises where the factory owners would want the cost to be reduced and not big manufacturers which allow corruption and do not need technology.

Business idea in Fintech

"Most banks will be made irrelevant by 2030."

Gartner

This headline caught my eyes today when I was reading Economic Times. ET quoted the above from Gartner Advisory -a leading financial advisory and consultant of the world. I was reading a lot on Fintech, Blockchain in media but this news was something awesome. I thought that I should understand the depth of fintech in India. I picked up the cell and called upon Anuj my friend who also happened to be the Executive Director of Ajcall Finance a Mumbai based listed NBFC.

I asked Anuj would it be a good idea if his offline NBFC company starts an online app for lending. I proposed him that an app can be developed which with the help of video KYC on a smartphone and OTP based signature of loan agreement can disburse personal loans instantaneously. Anuj told me that that there are more than 9, 000 NBFC in India and most of them are not clean and are not into active lending. Anuj told that though though have a NBFC license but they are not into active lending business as it involves a lot of regulatory compliances. He told me that the business model of his company is to arrange finances for SME and retail loans from banks and take a cut as processing charge which is a sure shot risk free approach to make money. He added that if he starts a lending fintech there are chances of failure which he can ill afford."

I said to myself that these NBFC which are around 9000 in number are not ready to change their business model as Anuj is unwilling. But they are oblivious of the fact that in the days to come the premium commanded by nbfc in secondary sale (to the tune of 30 lakhs or more) would diminish by the power of lending fintechs.

Not only valuation of NBFCs will reduce but that of of banks primarily focussed on retail banking segment is getting disrupted. Why would someone in future would like to go to a bank for any activity if app can replace whole banking activities. Then what good investment of banks in swanky plush, AC fitted large infrastructure would be needed. This cost would be huge to banks. Banks would then be left with wholesale banking targeting corporates which does not require huge physical infrastructure. Even tech companies like Indifi (started by Alok Mittal) and Kredx would snatch the revenue generated by banks in wholesale banking.

Banks gave way to ATMs, ATMs gave way to PayTM and paytm is paving way for PayTM bank.

HDFC chairman Mr Deepak Parikh announcing Rs 100 crore fund for investments in Fintech is perhaps the proof of his acknowledgement that he is able to see the writing on the wall.

Then I called another friend of his Mr Priush from Religare Finvest and threw my idea to start with me a fintech that would offer personal loans to people. But he said though he is a fintech enthusiast but he is not optimistic on possibilities for a new venture. He said when he thinks of mortgage loans, each of the property in India today is mortgaged. Then where is the scope of mortgage loans. And if retail loan is considered there are companies like Andromeda as aggregator. I further got enlightened that today a Andromeda sales person has reached every nook and corner of the country. Today such is the penetration that now when a loan is required in a remotest village, one approaches to a sarpanch and an andromeda sales guy is in close contact with sarpanch to get the loan disbursed.

So, there is no possibility of starting a mortgage loan or a new personal loan company.

"Then is there no scope for a new company to do business?"I was forced to think.

I realized that business is tough but definitely not to that extent that people are not starting afresh.

I took his advice with a pinch of salt and decided to move ahead with my plan.

Priush then introduced me to a new fintech startup just in case I may get some light on this business. This new fintech told me that they are making an app for distributing credit card. This company would make credit card DSA on app.

I wondered whether it is a right business model. **They were not creating any blue ocean in the name of fintech** as no new customer segment is formed.

Main Fintech Models are

1. Selling Mutual Funds on App like PayTM Money
2. Stock Trading on App like Zerodha

3. Personal Loan on App like MoneyTap, ZuluPay, ZestMoney

4. Payments-(Fiercely Competitive with VISA, PayTM, Google and Whatsapp in the fray)

5. Insurance

Amongst all the above fintech models a lending fintech gives the maximum return on investment. Lending Fintech space is disrupted with developments like landmark announcement of RBI to use video KYC and introduction of eNach and OTP based signing of loan agreement. This has allowed the lending fintechs to accept the loan application and disburse the loans almost instantaneously on app. This provides an abundant opportunity to Indian entrepreneurs.

Chapter 10

Confidentiality of Idea – NDA

A first time entrepreneur is mostly stuck in a quagmire on NDA (non disclosure agreement) thinking whether he should reveal his idea to anyone without signing an NDA or not.

The answer is "It depends. "

My Prof. Late Sh Ajit Prasad who taught us Strategy Management at IMI once gave us a valuable lesson in management which I still remember. He told us whenever something is being asked to you and you are not sure of the answer. Just say "It depends" and than you can bias your answer in any way.

But here when I mention whether to discuss your big idea with others or not and the answer is "It depends" is not a formula no IMI/Ajit Prasad/Formula no 2002. I really mean it here.

To have a correct view of your "imaginary big idea" or the hairy big audacious goal you need to discuss it with others and this is a prerequisite and you can not avoid sharing it with others. If you are not taking views of intellectuals you are doomed.

So, when to discuss and in what stage?

You can discuss your idea to a person who has no power of execution and safeguard it against a competitor or a corporation who in fraction of seconds can execute it.

By sharing your idea to others not only it will make your idea a sharper one but in return you may get a co-founder or investor or intern in the process

Yes at certain times NDA becomes necessary when one describes it to his competitors who can leverage it easily.

Chapter 11

VC Funding

———————————✦———————————

I continued telling my story to my friend,

I wanted to bring my business idea to life and needed funds to start, the media was flooded with stories of funding. There were so many VC's in India Sequoia, Matrix Partners, Blume Ventures, Ah! Ventures, Venture Catalysts.

Definitely I knew these all investors have big prerequisites to get investments from them. But I found many early stage platforms like Sequoia surge. Since I was having great ideas, I made business plans and darted them to VC's but was never able to raise funds. I wondered why? What makes VC's fund ideas.

My friend noted in the dairy,

"Naren, did not have any company, no product and most importantly no customers. He only has an idea and business plan and can he think of himself being investible?."

After making notes surreptitiously in his diary, my friend faced me and said tIhere is a reason why you are not funded.

You know Naren, VC's have the prerequisites before investing in a venture. These are

1. Team
2. Disruptive idea
3. Validation or proof of concept
4. Scalability
5. High Intellectual Property.
6. Pedigree of Top Tier colleges in India
7. The sector should be a virgin sunrise sector

Some VC's may even ask you to not marry or have a child (crazy it may seem) or even ask you to relocate yourself to their place. Some angels and VC's may also ask you who are the other investors and follow herd mentality. You have not left your day job or formed a team or have customers, then how do you think you qualify for even sitting across a VC.

Once they will fund you, they will want every piece of your flesh. They would want you to raise capital at every next round to give them an exit. They will make you run on your toes.

Are you ready for this capital, Naren?

It is a tradeoff of your existing zone of comfort. Only if you take risk, you may get the coveted next orbit. And then also you can not be sure of getting in the next orbit.

"After raising more than 40 million dollars for my various ventures, I still advise you to build your venture with no outside money."

Ankur Warikoo, CEO of Nearbuy -a PayTM invested company said while sharing his perspective on raising funds.

Do you know why many startups fail. Because they start with funding in mind.

And what happens is when you go to a VC without a product or without a team or without revenue, you end up mostly with no fundraising and loss of valuable time and energy.

And even if you are able to raise funds for your startup, your bargaining power in term sheet(a document showing intent of equity investment in a venture) decreases. VC put riders in term sheet in their favour and marginalize your interest. After raising the first round of funding you are forced to raise subsequent rounds of funding (as this is the only way that the existing investors get to have an exit). And growth (topline) takes precedence over bottomline and the entrepreneurs starts losing focus on basics of business i. e bringing profit into pockets as they have enough VC money in pockets.

Here are three examples which underlines the theory of bargaining with investors.

Rahul Yadav founded a real estate online venture named **Housing. com** and was successful in getting funded by Softbank. But since he raised funding too early, his decision making in the venture was governed largely by the investors. And he couldn't run the company the way he wanted and was finally thrown out by the investors.

Whereas if you start your entrepreneurial journey by first raising funds and then forming a team, product and bringing traction, your investors will dominate you.

Another case in the view is of VG Sidharth CEO of Cafe Coffee Day. He was a successful entrepreneur but had to take extreme steps owing to the pressure of private equity players. Hope you now understand the pressure after you raise funds and are building a business.

As per media reports, Rahul accused his investors of poaching talent from his venture Housing. com to their other venture companies. He further stated that he wants to distribute wealth to his colleagues working with them by way of hefty ESOPS. This reportedly irked his investors which forced them to fire Rahul unceremoniously.

Whereas the following case shows what benefits an entrepreneur reaps when he raises funds after building a team and having a good customer base.

Amit Jain of Car Dekho still owns a majority of share holding(around 60 percent) in the company even after huge investments from the likes of Sequoia in his venture. His company is growing healthily and probably he has less pressure from investors to raise next round as against where investors own more than 60 % in equity.

I said,

You are right, one should not take money from investors.

My friend said,

You are partly true. you should bootstrap first and after creating a sufficient traction, the path of funding becomes a bit easier. One should not be averse to VC funds as it may open new avenues but as it is said with immense power comes immense responsibility.

VC funds are like steroids and if taken in a metered dose works like a medicine but when you are intoxicated with a high dose, the withdrawal takes a heavy toll not only on your venture but also on you as well.

VC ke bharose na baithiye

Manjhi: The Mountain Man (2015) is a famous movie of a man who single handedly carves path from a mountain.

"Bhagwan Ke Bharose Na Baithiye, kya pata bhagwan hamare bharose baitha ho."

If you will keep on waiting for external investment and then start, you never will be able to start.

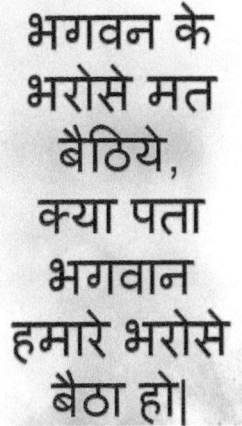

Lessons

Start a thing which you can sustain and you can finish. Make sure your idea is doable. The game should depend upon you. And not on investor.

For funding your business, VC's should be the last option. If those investors are not convinced with any of the above answers, go to your real investors -your customers. And just do it.

If your EBITDA is positive, VC will come to you rather you go on a hunting spree for you.

Yes it is tough for a startup, but keep your revenue flow positive and hunt for positive investors parallely (those who do not disturb in execution)

Case Study

MakeMyTrip an online travel company which has acquired many online travel companies the likes of which are IBIBO, Redbus, MyGola, HolidayIQ, Bitla Software and Quest2Travel.

Noteworthy is the investment of MakeMyTrip in Quest2Travel -a corporate travel booking tool company. Quest 2 Travel was founded in year 2000 (the same year in which Makemytrip was founded). Quest 2 Travel is founded by Mr Abhay Rangnekar. When I asked Mr Rangekar while writing this book on whether his company was profitable at time of acquisition.

He proudly replied to me,

"Yes, Founded the company in 2000. Got our 1st client in 2007. Started breaking even on day to day operations in 2010 and have been profitable every year since then. Retained all earnings and never withdrew profits. Used own money and owned 100 % shares before now selling a majority stake.

There is never a problem for a bootstrapped company which turns itself into a profit making company without any external investors. And the investors like Makemytrip will come all the way long to acquire you. Also to note it took him full 20 years to bootstrap his company. That is the grit and determination which an entrepreneur has to think before embarking on this path devoid of risk capital.

Lessons

1. Use your own funds to build business as far as possible (bootstrap).

2. Never withdraw money from business. You can afford only minimum salaries.

3. Avoid the lure of risk capital (VC money) and try to grow organically. This is a sure shot sign of success.

4. If you are gunning at B2C business, there are all chances that you would need the VC capital wherethe perils come along.

Questions you should ask to a VC

There are certain questions even an entrepreneur should ask an investor before taking their money like:-

1. Is the investor in position to do follow up round in case if needed.

2. How good the mentoring and networking help was given to their earlier portfolio companies.

But today in the race of raising funds, often entrepreneurs do not have bargaining power to discuss these questions.

Chapter 12

Cofounder

If you want to go fast, go alone. If you want to go far, go together

The co-founder is a person with whom you tie your one foot and try to run together.

I don't think that only an equity holder can be termed as a co-founder. But an investor harps that a co-founder should have a good equity holding while he doles out money to you.

In fact you will find some very wise investors giving gyan how much equity your cofounder must have before you approach an investor. They say a mere 5-7 % is to a cofounder shows it is given to him just to show and the equity holding by a cofounder should be optimally 15-20 %.

You will understand yourself that till one stage in your venture, you will not need a co-founder and time only will tell you when you need a co-founder. Once you start your journey you may find many people suitable to be your co-founders.

Throughout my life, I searched on linkedin, social media and even flew twice in a month just to meet a potential cofounder. But it bore no fruits and I couldn't find a cofounder.

Later on I realized, I was fooling in the name of entrepreneurship by vigorously searching for a cofounder and it was just a dart in the dark. Similar to flying without the wings.

I never started actually, never stood for myself, never tried to build a product or get customers and always thought that when someone will join me I will start.(Perhaps this was due to the fact that my mind was conditioned from VC talks who say they give preference to team before idea.

I waited for the right partner to begin my entrepreneurial journey.

That never happened.

It is your venture, don't look for a co-founder. Just start and see if you can ignite enough passion that people join your dream. Yes, this journey becomes easy when you are partnered with a co founder. But remember you will find a co-founder when you are a founder. So, start your journey. On the path you will find many who would be happy to join with the tag of a co-founder.

If you know someone with all the requisite skills and if he is the apt person to be your co founder, approach him. Rope him even if he is unable to invest. But if someone comes to join you as a co founder and you are not sure about the seriousness of that person then, please ask him to invest in the venture. So that he has his skin in the game.

I have observed that rarely would you come across people who have the same passion, the same zeal to match that of yours and rarely do you come across such stories. But you are told that funding is given to people who have a team. Is there any way out?

YES!! out solo and try to attract co-founders.

When people see the progress of your venture, it's easy to opt out for the right co founder. Take them in your fold and move on.

Never wait for a co-founder or VC to charter out. Charter out alone and you will find both.

Everyone wants to sit in a moving train. would you not do the same, when you are waiting for your co-founder's nod to join you or waiting for a seed fund. If you want to start, start right away.

Chapter 13

Jumping the Emotions

Now I had an idea (after much deliberation on what to do), understanding further not to approach any external investor, I was ready to jump the next orbit. But then I got stuck in sea of varied emotions.

During my engineering days and even in my late thirties I found that people behave differently even when they are treated evenly by me.

Off late, I made my life funda.

There are some negative people in society and there are some positive people in society.

Example 1

I will give you examples from my life.

There is a small kirana store across the corner of my home. Whenever my wife wanted something from the store and I used to run to the shop, my 6 year old daughter accompanied me. Whenever we were there at the shop, she used to play with packets of snacks and chocolate boxes and sometimes with this the sequence of some stocks at the counter got disturbed. Then the shopkeeper used to frown getting irritated would angrily reprimand my daughter "thek se khade raho" (stand properly).

This unruly behaviour pissed me off as I wondered why he does not understand that sometimes pampering customers gives more business.

I stopped going to that grocery shop. I started going to a shop which was little farther. This shopkeeper was an old wise business man.

My daughter easily went inside his shop daily and played with different grocery stuff. He never uttered a word. My daughter accessed over the counter and touched containers of sugar, pulses with the measuring tool. Instead of scolding her like the previous shopkeeper, this gentlemen always used to smile and even used to give a small toffee as a gift to her. I felt very happy.

I became a regular customer of his.

Don't think you can change someone by your positive thinking and benevolent actions. Leave them alone.

Example 2

There are many people whom I follow on linkedin. Many of these spread gyan to entrepreneurs like anything. And if you check them, they have never found anything worth pinching the salt.

Many of them call themselves "angels". What is amusing is that they do not have any portfolio.

I am not able to make out what kind of these angels are?

I started disliking this community so called investors. I started thinking when they have not even done a venture, is it rightful for them to call themselves as mentors.

But I have developed wisdom which may prove helpful to people who are on the scrambled path of life.

When you develop wisdom you understand that in this world there are some real angels and there are con people at the same time.

Chapter 14

Business Lessons

1. Branding, PR and Sales
2. Cash Flow

Branding, PR and Sales

PR means personal relations which is essentially cost free (unless one is hired for the job) which helps to promote a product or service.

A first time entrepreneur relives his imagination frequently of creating his brand a household name. Very often he gets swayed with the brand image of his product that he tends to overspend on PR and branding. In fact I imagined this and few times this overpowered my rationality in making decisions while allocating marketing budget. This paid PR gives a feeling to an entrepreneur that he has "arrived" after struggling for so many year. And he spends money on brand building rather than concentrating on sales. Wherein only sales keeps a bootstrapped venture alive. There is a difference between sales and marketing. Though marketing increases sales but not always as marketing involves brand building. And brand building pays in longer run. Whereas a startup venture needs to first cross the first 365 days which is the valley of death. And most of the startups die prematurely in the very first year due to unjustified expenditures which needs to be closely checked.

I have two good examples here.

1. In his words from Sahil Barua –CEO and Co Founder of Delhivery

   'A bad piece of advice that we got from our investors was that we should be a lot more visible in the media. We had just raised Series B and everyone recommended that we get out out there and do a huge PR push about what we were building. So, we spend about a year investing in PR only to realize there is literally no advantage in doing this.'

   Actually PR gives a feeling to first time entrepreneur that he has reached. His ego gets satisfied. He has been declined, refused and not accepted by his friends and family hence he wants to proclaim that he has made it. But actually it is of no use. Entrepreneurship is a journey. PR may bring recognition but not customers. Weigh ROI on PR viz a viz ROI on Facebook

   From How I almost blew it…. Sidharth Rao

2. Done card is a prepaid card company went to its destruction before it could grow. It sponsored a show on CNBC for 2 crores, which industry sources told me later on that it was a bolt from blue to a struggling startup and perhaps spearheaded their downfall.

(It is a different story that prepaid cards like Done card and ITZ cash card were outdated by smartphone payments due to technological evolution)

Bottomline is do not waste money on branding when you are a startup and focus on sales instead of marketing. Do branding when you comfortably can. Don't imagine your name of company to be a brand. That is why it takes some entrepreneurs so long (page no 85 of this book) to choose a domain name and are left with too little time to do the actual thing called SALES)

In your initial years of startup do not hire a PR agency or self branding company. As a startup, always aim at sales before branding.

Lesson

Cash Flow

You will never be out of business because of loss but because of mismanagement of cash flow and no cash in the bank.

Cash Flow is very important –Don't get trapped into lack of proper management and continuous flow of it. Release payments only when it is required and collect your receivables as soon as you can.

Chapter 15

Time: Taylor's Principle

Taylor' principle states that the work adjusts itself according to the time given. This essentially means that most of us never complete the work before the time alloted for the work and complete it only when the given time is over.

It is imperative that Entrepreneurs should understand the implications of this.

Very often then not entrepreneurs engage themselves in entrepreneurial activities assuming that they have infinite time which is actually not the case.

First time entrepreneurs devote endless time in

1. Choosing an idea to start a venture (They should instead select an idea within time frame and start executing which will build their confidence and can tweak the idea along the course of execution)

2. Choosing a domain name.

3. Making a logo (on which many entrepreneurs not only spend time unnecessarily but also money)

4. In launching their website or app (they want to make the app a perfect one and eventually lose time there, the goal should be to make a workable site and start.)

5. Raising funds (instead of building a venture by bootstrapping).

6. Waiting for a cofounder to start.

7. Drafting a business plan for getting loan form VC (instead of executing).

And more importantly first time entrepreneurs take too long a time to pivot or shut it down if things are not working. It would be a rational decision to shut down the project, if it's not working within stipulated time. Rather than hanging on emotionally to the idea.

Timing of what theme of idea to choose, when to raise funds, when to sell off your venture and when to shut down your venture if you are not succeeding is very important. Timing plays an important role.

In simpler terms define a timeline for your project. And complete it in that time.

This is for those people who do not share equity.

Build your startup as if you have only 3 years to build, nurture and sell it. Then only you will make fast decisions. Two years is a sufficient time to go through all the waves and up-and-downs of business and be seasoned to run the show. At the end of this period you should be in position to decide whether to continue or shutdown and move to the next venture.

When you are embarking upon your journey,

You will end up wasting time choosing a domain name, which name is good or relevant and whether domain name relates or conveys the message of your business idea. These things do not matter that much to the success of your venture.

You may end up taking endless time to fix all features of your software before you give it to your software vendor to configure because you want to incorporate all the features and want to do no manual work and want to do it fully automated robust platform.

After your software is built you want it to be perfect before the site goes live, without forgetting the fact that you have limited time for each activity.

You may wait for an investor endlessly before you start and execute your startup because of your thinking that you have enough time.

You may be waiting to have some revenue before you send the bplan to an investor as you know investors invest only when there is revenue on books.

You may be waiting for support to come from your wife, family before you get validation.

You may keep on waiting for an investor who gives you a better valuation, when you already have one proposition in hand.

You may keep on waiting for a co-founding member who agrees for a less equity stake.

This all may not happen at one stroke for most.

This all may happen in the dream world of utopia, so be pragmatic and allocate optimum time to each activity and adhere to it.

People will only support you when you show them the result.

This is all virality.

The only way to win over this whole vicious circle is fix a time for each activity and move on.

Allocate time for each activity.

Make a bplan for yourself. Divide your goals into yearly goals and then monthly goals and then fix a daily routine and convert your daily goal to daily actionable steps which can be monitored and metered.

Like, for choosing a domain name one should not take more than 4 hours.

Remember start backwards –Think like this. You have to build your business in 3 years and sell it and come out of it.

Life is not endless. You don't have infinite time at your hand (That does not mean you work hard against time, you don't need to work on your lappie even when you reach home or be on phone when your wife is ready with dinner on hand and you are busy(this is not time management).

It is easier said than done. But practice it and you will master it. Take daily notes of yourself and ask, are you able to train your mind to say to yourself that entrepreneurship is not the be all and end all.

Just take fast decisions, go with whatever you have and wherever you are. This will keep you grounded and you will be able to make better decisions.

Fail Fast. Learn Fast. Get up fast. Fail Again. Learn Fast. Get up again. Repeat

Don't wait.

Who selected the name Infosys and on what basis was it chosen?

Narayan Muthy "When we decided to start the company on December 29, 1980. I chose N. S. Raghavan, Kris Gopalakrishnan and Nandan Nilekani to work with me. I asked them to think of a name. Generally, I am a very impatient person. So, I told tIm that they had to come back to me with a name in 48 hours or I would choose a name. For some reason they did not come back with a name. Therefore, I chose the name."

Such is "Business @ speed of thought" Bill Gates talks about. Do not hang around issues for long.

You need to define time for each activity.

Chapter 16

How to Overcome Self Doubt, Fear and Pain

Self Doubt

Today was a very hectic day of mine at office. Not only because of the routine office tasks but it was because of the same thoughts and worries that ran in my mind. I was in the dilemma whether to put the whole savings of my life at risk by investing in a venture, the outcome of which is not sure. I was debilitating in my mind again whether I am taking a right step, by even thinking of leaving my job. I was talking to myself about how I can think of selling my flat whose EMI is still going on when other friends at my age of 40 plus are in process of buying a next property.

I was really shaken and filled with fear and got scared.

What if I am not able to get the desired results from my action.

How will my family survive?

I again thought of taking help from my dear friend vikas,

My friend commented,

Do you know Naren, that in India 83 % of the workforce would prefer to quit jobs to become an entrepreneur as per a survey by Randstad. But for people to become entrepreneurs, it doesn't need money (as VC money) you think of, it needs nerves of steel. If it wouldn't have been the case then everyone can become an entrepreneur. Everybody is not able to overcome self doubt, fear and has the courage to take risks.

Guilt

Today when I returned from office by mistake I left out a hardcopy of business plan on my table in the study room. And I realized this when my wife yelled on me "once again a business plan, I can not tolerate you any more. You just keep on making business plans but except wasting money you are good for nothing."

I patiently told her how I can do business being on the job.

She said, "When you know this then why do you spend money on a business plan. Stick to your job."

How can I explain to her that entrepreneurship is natural to me?

And I have suppressed it for many years.

I thought to make her understand this but chose to keep quiet to maintain the yoga (balance) of the house.

I thought she was not able to understand me.

But then something happened which forced me to rethink "am I able to understand her".

My eyes got stuck on the water dripping out of the refrigerator in the house. And I was feeling low and in guilt. The refrigerator was decades old and water coming out of it was an unserviceable problem. The house needed a new fridge which I was avoiding as I was putting every penny of money I earned into my entrepreneurship dream.

I was in guilt. In my pursuit to entrepreneurship, I was ignoring the basic needs of my family.

I am a mortal and I sometimes lose the power to control my emotions.

Trying to forget the above episode I regained composure and dialed one of my MBA classmate who I thought was a "friend". She did not take my call and avoided me as she has been doing. I just needed her advice on finance domain. Not only she but all of my "friends" started avoiding me.

I tried to figure out if there was something wrong in seeking help.

Why I am so hell bent to bring misery to me and my family.

I was having guilt and filled with remorse and self doubt, contemplating am I addicted to such activities which I call entrepreneurial to just keep my adrenaline pumping.

I thought I am a sinner. I have committed sins.

Pain

It is painful because I tried and after so many years I haven't received any results yet.

I called my friend and said the journey of life is very painful. Whenever I got tired of not getting results, I sat and started wondering, have I done something wrong. I ponder for hours why I haven't reached. What mistake I'm doing, is my path correct?

He said mockingly, "don't you know -No pain no gain". If you can not bear it, better be out of this.

For every ailment under the sun,

There is a remedy or there is none,

If there is one, try to find it,

If there is none, just ignore it.

My friend noted

"Nobody is destined to reach anywhere. Life is just a journey."

His words were falling on my deaf ears. Perhaps I did not want pep talks. I was thinking aloud, in my inclination towards entrepreneurship, I have lost friends who now don't even pick my phone, my wife thinks of me as an insane person. Why I m on a path which is bringing miseries to everybody.

But Vikas nudged me and broke my chain of thoughts saying "Naren you think you are suffering because your pain has no equal in the world. But you are oblivious of the fact that people have pains which they can not even share." They are able to withstand pain because they understand that pain is inevitable and they know that **"this too shall pass"** and never worry about results.

I told my friend that it is still painful.

He asked me what is causing you pain?

I continued,

"There are unfulfilled desires which are causing pain. I dreamt of making it big, to bring an IPO and open the listing by ringing a bell at the stock exchange. I dreamt of creating a brand but I am not able to walk even a small lane on the big path and suffered a lot."

He said,

You are not happy now, as you say you will be happy in the next higher orbit but I am telling you that you will never be satisfied.

Ask yourself if you attain the power, the glory, the wealth you aspire would you be happy.

Not sure?

My friend said, "I told you life and entrepreneurship is a journey and not a destination.

In Mahabharat Arjun confessed to Lord Krishna that to battle against his own relatives, he feels weak at heart. He even asked Lord Krishna to fight the battle along with him. To this, Krishna said, "I can tell you the path but you have to walk".

One needs to train his mind.

Everyday a entrepreneur will face denials and rejections. He may need a small "udhaar" from friends, he may need a small piece of advice from his old batch mates who are in good position in finance and technology sector. Tie-ips will not be happening. Your wife will be nagging, you will not be accepted. You will not be able to raise funds. You will not be able to buy fancy furniture.

Those failures are bound to happen.

Naren you have to develop your nerves of steel.

Your mind will play many games with you. The beauty of mind is that it always contradicts the present state and always opposes the decision you have made or you are going to make.

Let your life be unfazed by any positive or negative thoughts.

Don't let a positive reply from an investor oversway your thoughts. No exhilaration, No depression.

When you get a positive reply from an investor, don't go over the roof to shout to your surroundings, perhaps the cheque may never come. And when your surroundings will ask you on your success, you will not have any answer.

My friend said,

Let me share with you the life of those entrepreneurs who lost it when they were at the zenith of their business. If they did not complain and can start once again their journey of entrepreneurship, you have no right to whine who has not even started it.

Vaitheeswaran of Fabmart was thrown out of competition despite being a pioneer in ecommerce.

Alok Kejriwal of contest2win was forcibly removed out of his venture.

Darshan Patel who founded the famous Krack Cream had to leave the company he founded.

The legendary Steve Jobs was kicked out of Apple.

Vaitheeswaran

Vaithee, as people fondly call him, founded Fabmart which is India's first e-Commerce site. The venture was known as first Fabmart and then Fabmall and then Indiaplaza which was later on acquired by Aditya Birla group and rebranded as More Stores which eventually was bought over by Amazon. Even when you will find such big names attached. I am putting some excerpts from his autobiography for you to understand what it takes to build a venture successfully and yet fail in life.

"On 15th September 2008, Lehman brothers filed for bankruptcy and I was told by the investors that no further money will be available

for Indiaplaza and you have to manage on your own. Business went down and employees started quitting. Vendors suddenly became a deluge to recover dues.

A merchant in Mumbai who owed around Rs 3 lakh by Indiaplaza knew someone in Mumbai who knew someone at the 'top' in Bengaluru police circles. This someone told the Ulsoor police station cops to investigate the case. When I escalated this dire situation to the investors and directors, I was advised to run away with my family and check into a hotel as the cops could arrest me on Friday night to ensure I spend the weekend behind bars.

One employee posted that my wife should be gang raped to teach me a lesson. Another employee threatened to commit suicide and name me as the cause of his death in his suicide letter if I did not pay his salary dues.

Select merchants deliberately started calling daily after midnight asking for payments.

I emailed the investors requesting them to settle the dues and properly shut down the company but there was no response.

This founder started thinking of evading such circumstances by disguising even after 14 years of running the company.

The company was established, had a team, was adequately venture funded with good brand name but couldn't sustain after the onslaught of Amazon and Flipkart in India.

Did his business mathematics of making profits in a business went wrong. In his own words in his book "Ask me" and he replies in tears what the trauma is when you have reached the finishing line you are declared not fit and not eligible for the race.

Naren, in your opinion what this guy should do with life.

Vaithee understands this and despite his miseries, he has once again started a new venture named 'Again Drinks' at the age of 56 years. He is as joyful as ever to start his second innings.

Here Vaithee was lucky enough to be not put behind the bars, I recall Yogendra Vasupal founder of Stayzilla was put behind bars since his company failed to pay the dues which should have invoked civil case instead of criminal case. That is the clout of money. No investors turned up for his help.

You have to be ready for such a thing, if you say you want to be an entrepreneur.

Sometimes in entrepreneurship, you will do all the things, reach there but will still be left out. That is the game.

Darshan Patel

Darshan Patel is the man behind building the brand Krack cream. It was unfortunate that due to family feud he had to leave his company that he built.

He took the challenge and left the company to once again build a successful company Vini Cosmetics which is popularly known as Fogg Deo.

Alok Kejriwal

Alok Kejriwal, built his company Mobile2Win a mobile marketing company from nowhere facing a lot of hurdles. But he was forced to leave the same company that he founded when Norwest Venture Partners acquired Mobile2win. com in India on the condition that Kejriwal would exit.

Alok bounced back from the failure to build now games2win -a mobile gaming company.

Just imagine, you conceive a baby which you long yearned for but have to leave for the good sake of the baby. The pain such situations creates in your life is tremendous.

Nothing is permanent. Even winning is not permanent. So, do not worry.

Vaitheeswaran, Alok Kejriwal, Darshan Patel, Steve Jobs all of them were toppled in their business which they once built but they knew how to handle failure and bounced back. The pain they endured never deterred them to start again. When you start for an ambition, you should know that you may not be successful in your first attempt despite your full throttle. This knowledge gives you tremendous power to bounce back again and again.

Nothing is permanent so don't lament if you havent reached or arrived yet.

Lesson

The Resurrection

After several attempts and learning valuable lessons along the way. I went into slumber to de-stress and rethink about my entrepreneurial journey. I decided to attempt mental and bodily cleansing. I decided to stop reading newspapers, books and digital articles. I replaced my smart phone with only a call and message feature phone for one month. To check whether entrepreneurship is an impulsive decision for me. With the help of yoga and destress techniques, I was able to calm my impulses and develop focus. I was lucky enough to achieve a great amount of calmness and equanimity in myself. Then came the time to face the real challenge of my life.. I decided to face the idea of entrepreneurship again. I went through all the ideas and the research I had done. But this time it was different. My entrepreneurial spirit had the strength of my equanimous mind.

I thought that I will take the things as they come and do not overthink. I will not worry about the investor any more.

Following lines started floating in my mind

If it comes, let it.

If it goes, let it.

As I was lost in my thoughts my wife came into the room with my phone in her hand and murmured "there is a call for you, I have not picked up but it is showing some mausa ji of yours in its display name."

I took the phone and smiled at her after looking at it as the phone was from Masayoshi of Softbank.

It is Japan calling.

Next Orbit: De-Stress Techniques

The following are a few of the practical de-stress techniques which helped me to overcome emotional turmoil. Hope this will relieve some of it for you also.

1. Go for a jog regularly morning or evening –Not only for health benefits, but it removes negativity also.

2. Talk to a person whom you feel you are close to when you think the society is not understanding you and you are all alone to make a decision.

3. Listen to your favourite music.

4. Have a break with your family or take a small vacation. And if you can't take small family breaks, don't stop yourself from taking a sunbath at the terrace of your house. Those happy moments are yours. The glory, the fame you visualize may come, may not come or may come and go.

5. Nutrition, sleep, reading, enjoying sunshine aimlessly, hearing the songs of birds and the evening walk will bring you in sync with nature.

6. Practice Yoga.

YOGA-The powerful way to do KARMA without attaching any strings to it.

What is yoga?

Is Yoga just a 30-40 minutes aasan and dhyan you do daily in the morning or in the evening

No.

Yoga is to be practiced every minute of the day. How?

Yoga means sum total. And the sum total of nature always remains the same. Yoga is "yog" –the sum total. It is the sum total of all the feelings of the human beings. Nothing is created and nothing is destroyed. Only one form of energy changes into another. Similarly happiness, sadness, guilt, anger, depression, dejection, jealousy all are natural but when they take over you, they will harm you. So what to do. As soon as you realize do not get angry, have no guilt, feel no joy or remorse.

You get a firing from your boss, you sadden, your leave not sanctioned, you sadden, your wife nags you on your failure, you sadden.

Yoga is balance yoga is equilibrium. If you are workaholic, kick yourself and bring yourself at par.

Little difficult it may be, but not impossible at all.

Try it.

Yoga is about mastering your mind.

Mind is like a monkey which is drunken and jumps on one twig to another twig of a tree. So uncontrollable is he mind.

A human mind is like that only. It gets provoken on slightest stimulus.

Anxiety is natural and it will crawl and try to grip your mind.

Guilt is natural. Control it. you become yogi.

Anger is natural but control your anger.

You may ask —why to control emotions.

Being ecstatic on the news that an investor is receptive to your business idea is fine. But you will note when the same investor changes his mood last minute it will give you jitters. Had you trained your mind, not to feel buoyant on this note of getting investment the rejection will never grip you.

Pain, anger, sadness, guilt, happiness, ecstasy, pessimism are all emotions we experience all the time in a day. It's better to regulate these emotions.

Don't get carried away by them.

Guilt, pain and fear are all weaknesses, which stops you from doing your rightful duty.

Entrepreneurial Power Capsules

Envision and execute on your own capabilities and don't rely on others expertise.

Lessons summarized for an entrepreneur

1. If you seek early validation, early approval on your efforts as an entrepreneur for your idea, you will never succeed.

2. Invest your money first.

3. VC aur Co-founder kay bharose mat bathiyay.

4. Start the venture in your own city.

5. Build virality in your model (through B2B / franchise or whatsoever)

6. Best model today in tech entrepreneurship is to build a tech platform and earn fixed money from it from clients(like software products).

7. Don't get carried away to start an entrepreneurship in the field of passion. You have to weigh it, if it is doable/ feasible. Doable is what you can execute and feasible is what makes economic sense. The other word for feasible

on a large scale is scalable. In short a thing which you can start small and take on to a large scale through technology.

8. Never share your business or life secrets with anybody.

9. Network with people extensively-THE PEOPLE YOU MEET ARE YOUR DOTS, THEY WILL HELP YOU.

10. Build your business brick by brick, one step at a time – Kiran Mazumdar Founder of Biocon

11. IP or no IP, it does not matter, if you are a first time entrepreneur.

12. Team or no team does not matter (everybody joins when a feast is served but not for preparing it). In fact investor is a team and co-founder is a team. Don't try to drag them. They will join when you are successful.

13. Take care of your physical and mental health.(Let me check for you. You score zero if you leave office after 6 p. m., and score another zero if you are on mobile after reaching home, and negative if you neglect your family on Sundays. Detox whatsapp, business calls at home or it will have a heavy toll on your life.

14. B2B or B2C-never mind (until they are profit making. Just do dhandha. Leave b2b, b2c for investors to estimate). But prefer not to build a b2c business where every time you need a new customer.

15. Internet based ideas are present and future.

16. Don't try to change consumer habits as evangelism takes time and money.(unless if you have deep pockets)

17. Talk about your project to people (never ask about nda, do not fear).

18. Entrepreneurship /life /career is a cycle –come out of it as soon as you can and try to jump to the next orbit. Don't hang to your first failure. You have to test 99 bulbs to understand how to make 100 th bulb lit.

19. Don't be on steroids of VC money for long.-You may become a media darling overnite and admired by your family but there is a price for it. If you are ready for the consequence of this dope called VC money then only go for it.

20. Start a venture when you have capital for one year otherwise you would lose the little capital which you have put.

21. If you look around ideas, there are umpteen, you will find only one on which you can bet your life.

22. You may post or ping on Linkedin /Barcamps/Startup event to find a co-founder but seldom it will bore fruits unless and until you start and give some momentum or bring traction to the idea.

23. Stand up first for yourself. Invest yourself and if you are on job, then first leave your job and become an engine, then only the bogeys(investors, family, cofounder) will join you.

24. It may be necessary for a VC to consider your cofounder as an equity holder whereas if you are building your business without the risk capital, this is not the case.

25. Never take personal loans for investment in shares.

26. Don't do a startup which is manpower intensive.

27. Attempt a business which is tech based and asset light.

28. Build a thing for the future.

29. Build a platform company rather than a fulfillment company.

30. Always make sure that the business you are into has profits and is scalable.

31. Find a unorganized market (Read Book :Blue Ocean Strategy)

Books

Following are the power booster books for your perusal, specially curated for you.

> Some books are to be read, some to be chewed and others to be assimilated.
>
> **Mahatma Gandhi.**

Books I assimilated

Every line of the following books makes sense and can be read twice.

1. Why I stopped wearing my Socks by Alok Kejriwal-It is the best business book I have read.

2. Business maharajas by Geeta Piramal

3. Entrepreneur's soul book by Swati Jena-This is a practical book which teaches not to leave your job in haste. And it advocates that to jump to the next orbit, one should have a strong footing in the present orbit.

4. Entrepreneurial Genius by Jessica Livingston–This book formed the foundation of my thought that if you have to jump the next orbit fast, take life as Taylor's principle (explained in this book).

5. Body Language by Allan Pease –I still use this book in my day to today life.

6. Who moved my cheese by Spencer Johnson.

7. Ocean blue strategy by W. Chan Kim.

8. Porter strategy –always be on the lookout to lock your competitor.

Books I chewed

1. Fountainhead-It shapes your individuality-If you have patience to read this bulky book, you will discover that there is YOU –which is different from the world. This individuality is discussed in this book.

2. Guide to investing-I couldn't find the basics of investing as anticipated by me in this book.

Message to Entrepreneurs from Shrimad Bhagvad Geeta

Arjun was confused while fighting the battle against his own relatives that he asked Lord Krishna to enlighten him.

Lord Krishan said,

"Arjun, you are confused and are fearful of whether you are doing the right thing to fight against your own relatives because you think you will be responsible for the consequences of your actions. You fail to understand that you are merely a doer and you can not claim the outcome of your actions, be it joy or sorrow.

It is me who is doing all your deeds. The moment you realize this, that only God has done deeds through and you need not worry- you will relax."

मन्मना भव मद्भक्तो मद्याजी मां नमस्कुरु ।
मामेवैष्यसि युक्त्वैवमात्मानं मत्परायण: ॥ 34॥

Always think of Me, be devoted to Me, worship Me, and offer obeisance to Me. Having dedicated your mind and body to Me, you will certainly come to Me.

Shri Bhagvat Gita.

This is the large me. Surrender yourself to me and I shall take care of you. Dedicate your every karma to me and you will have no fear.

References

How I almost Blew it by Sidharth Rao

Failing to Succeed by K. Vaitheeswaran

Why I stopped wearing my socks by Alok Kejriwal

An excerpt from Dare Magazine December 2010 issue.